100 facts

Astronomy

100 facts

Astronomy

Sue Becklake

Consultant: Steve Parker

Miles Kelly

First published in 2011 by Miles Kelly Publishing Ltd
Harding's Barn, Bardfield End Green, Thaxted, Essex, CM6 3PX, UK

Copyright © Miles Kelly Publishing Ltd 2011

This edition printed in 2012

4 6 8 10 9 7 5 3

Publishing Director Belinda Gallagher
Creative Director Jo Cowan
Editorial Director Rosie McGuire
Volume Designers Jo Cowan, Andrea Slane
Image Manager Liberty Newton
Indexer Eleanor Holme
Production Manager Elizabeth Collins
Reprographics Anthony Cambray, Stephan Davis
Assets Lorraine King

ISBN 978-1-84810-472-3

Printed in China

British Library Cataloguing-in-Publication Data
A catalogue record for this book is available from the British Library

ACKNOWLEDGEMENTS
The publishers would like to thank the following artists who have contributed to this book:
Julian Baker, Mike Foster (Maltings Partnership), Alex Pang, Rocket Design, Mike Saunders
All other artwork from the Miles Kelly Artwork Bank

The publishers would like to thank the following sources for the use of their photographs:
t = top, b = bottom, l = left, r = right, c = centre, bg = background
Cover: Detlev Van Ravenswaay/Science Photo Library

Corbis 15(c) Araldo de Luca; 29(tl) IAC/GTC **Dreamstime** 24(c) Kramer-1; 32(t) Silverstore **Fotolia.com** 10(l) Sharpshot;
21(tl) Georgios Kollidas, (r) Konstantin Sutyagin; 24(tc) pdtnc; 24–25(bg) Jenny Solomon; 44(clockwise from bl) Stephen Coburn,
Petar Ishmeriev, pelvidge, Mats Tooming **iStockphoto** 20–21(bg) Duncan Walker; 21(br) Steven Wynn; 22(cr) Steven Wynn;
23(br) Steven Wynn; 24(tl) HultonArchive; 25(tc) Duncan Walker **NASA** 8(bl) GReatest Images of NASA (NASA-HQ-GRIN),
(br) NASA Goddard Space Flight Center (NASA-GSFC); 9(tl) NASA Jet Propulsion Laboratory (NASA-JPL); 10–11 NASA-JPL;
12(cr) NASA-JPL; 13(clockwise from cl) NASA-JPL, NASA-HQ-GRIN, NASA-JPL, NASA-JPL; 22(bl) NASA-JPL;
24(cl) NASA-HQ-GRIN, (bc) NASA-JPL, (br) NASA-JPL; 29(br) NASA-JPL; 34–35(c) NASA-JPL; 35(tr) NASA Marshall Space Flight
Center (NASA-MSFC), (bl) NASA-JPL; 39(tl) NASA-JPL, (c) NASA-MSFC; 42(br) NASA-JPL; 43(cr) NASA-JPL, (br) NASA-JPL
Photolibrary.com 18–19 Steve Vidler **Rex** 27(cr) Nils Jorgensen **Science Photo Library** 6–7 J-P Metsavainio; 8–9 Chris Cook;
16(bl) Royal Astronomical Society; 17(tl) Detlev Van Ravenswaay; 18(tr) Eckhard Slawik; 20(bc) Dr Jeremy Burgess,
(br) Royal Astronomical Society; 20–21(t) NYPL/Science Source; 21(cl); 22–23(tc); 24(tr) Richard J. Wainscoat, Peter Arnold inc.;
26–27(tc) J-P Metsavainio; 30 David Nunuk; 31(tr) Adam Hart-Davis; 32–33(b) Christian Darkin; 33(tr) Dr Jean Lorre;
36–37 Peter Menzel; 37(br) NRAO/AUI/NSF; 39(br) NASA; 40–41(bl) Mark Garlick, (tl) NASA/WMAP Science Team,
(cr) NASA/ESA/STSCI/R.Williams, HDF-S Team; 44–45 Frank Zullo; 45(tl) Detlev Van Ravenswaay, (tr) Tony & Daphne Hallas;
46(r) NASA/Regina Mitchell-Ryall, Tom Farrar; 47(tr) European Space Agency, (cr) European Space Observatory
Shutterstock 9(tr) martiin||fluidworkshop; 10–11(label graphic) clickthis; 11(tr) Shawn Hine; 12–13(screen graphic) Linali;
14(cl) caesart; 15(br) Gordon Galbraith; 19(cr) Alex Hubenov; 24(tl frame) RDTMOR; 25(l) jordache; 27(bg) Vlue; 31(b) H. Damke;
39(tr) Dmitry Nikolajchuk

All other photographs are from:
PhotoDisc, Flat Earth

Made with paper from a sustainable forest

www.mileskelly.net   info@mileskelly.net

www.factsforprojects.com

CONTENTS

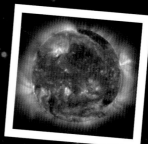

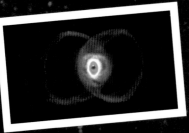

What is astronomy?

1 Astronomy is the study of everything you can see in the night sky and many other things out in space. Astronomers try to find out all about stars and galaxies. They look for planets circling around stars, and at mysterious explosions far out in space. Telescopes help them to see further, spotting things that are much too faint to see with just their eyes.

▼ New stars are forming in this cloud of dark dust and glowing gas in space. It is called the Pelican Nebula.

Families of stars

2 **Stars are huge balls of hot gas.** They look tiny to us because they are so far away. Deep in the centre of a star it is so hot that some of the gas turns into energy. Stars shine by sending out this energy as light and heat.

3 **A star starts life in a cloud of dust and gas called a nebula.** Thicker parts of the cloud collapse into a ball that becomes a star. Sometimes a star will shine until its gas is used up, and then swell into a red giant star. A large star may then explode as a supernova but smaller ones just shrink, becoming tiny white dwarf stars.

A star's colour shows how hot it is. Red stars are small and cool, yellow ones are bigger and hotter, and white ones are huge and very hot. Dying stars get even bigger, becoming giants or supergiants.

▶ The Milky Way Galaxy looks like a band of light, instead of a spiral shape, because we are looking through it from inside one of the spiral arms.

BUTTERFLY NEBULA

At the end of its life a red giant star threw out this glowing cloud of gas.

STAR CLUSTER

The Quintuplet cluster is a group of bright young stars. They shine with different colours – red, blue and white.

M81 GALAXY

This huge spiral galaxy contains billions of stars. Our Milky Way Galaxy would look like this if we could see it from above.

5 **Galaxies are huge families of stars.** Some are shaped like squashed balls, and these are called elliptical galaxies. Others have a spiral shape with arms curling out from a central ball of stars. Our Sun is in a spiral galaxy called the Milky Way. On very clear, dark nights you can see it as a faint band of light across the sky.

6 **Using powerful telescopes, astronomers can see galaxies in all directions.** They think there are many billions of galaxies, each containing billions of stars. All these stars and galaxies are part of the Universe. This is the name we give to everything we know about, including all the galaxies, our Sun and Moon, the Earth and everything on it, including you.

Our place in space

NEPTUNE

URANUS

SATURN

JUPITER

7 **The Sun is our nearest star.** It is an average-sized, medium-hot yellow star. From Earth, the Sun looks bigger than all other stars because it is much nearer. Without the Sun's light and heat nothing could live on Earth.

▶ Light from the Sun lets us see the planets and moons, which do not make their own light — we see them because the Sun's light bounces off them.

8 **A family of planets circles the Sun on paths called orbits.** This is called the Solar System. Near the Sun are four smaller planets called Mercury, Venus, Earth and Mars. Further out are four big ones called Jupiter, Saturn, Uranus and Neptune. They all travel at different speeds and spin as they go.

Asteroid belt

◀ There are thousands of big asteroids and probably millions of smaller ones.

9 All the planets except Mercury and Venus have moons circling them. Mars has two tiny ones. Earth has one large Moon – a round rocky ball with no air. The giant planets all have large families of moons – Jupiter and Saturn have over 60 each. Some of these are large, like our Moon, but most are small and icy.

MAKE A MOBILE
You will need:
card   scissors
colouring pencils   string
paper plate   sticky tape

1. Cut out nine circles of card, some big and some small, to be the planets and the Sun.
2. Colour the circles to look like the Sun and planets.
3. Use string and tape to hang the circles from the plate.
4. Hang your mobile from string stuck to the other side of the plate.

SUN

MARS

Earth's moon

EARTH

VENUS

MERCURY

10 Asteroids are chunks of rock, and are also part of the Solar System. Most of them circle the Sun between Mars and Jupiter in a band called the asteroid belt. Astronomers are always on the lookout for asteroids that might hit the Earth.

11 Comets come from the cold outer parts of the Solar System. They are made of dust and ice. When a comet nears the Sun, some of the ice melts and forms a glowing tail, which shines brightly until it moves away again.

Planets large and small

12 **Mercury is the smallest planet and closest to the Sun.** This rocky ball is very hot during the day, but freezing at night because it has no air to hold heat. Venus is about the same size as Earth. It is covered with clouds that trap heat so it is even hotter than Mercury.

EARTH
Length of day: 24 hours
Length of year: 365 days
Special features: Earth is the only planet where life is known to exist

MARS
Length of day: 24.6 Earth hours
Length of year: 687 Earth days
Special features: The largest volcano in the Solar System, called Olympus Mons

▶ Mars has ice caps in the far north and south, like the Arctic and Antarctic on Earth.

MERCURY
Length of day: 59 Earth days
Length of year: 88 Earth days
Special features: Many craters made by space rocks crashing into the planet billions of years ago

VENUS
Length of day: 243 Earth days
Length of year: 225 Earth days
Special features: Thick atmosphere pressing down so hard it would crush any visiting astronaut

▼ Venus has volcanoes all over its surface. This one, called Maat Mons, is the tallest.

13 **The planet we live on — Earth — is the third planet from the Sun.** It is mostly covered with water and it has air, both of which living things need to survive, so all kinds of animals and plants can thrive here. Mars is the furthest of the small rocky planets from the Sun. Its dry surface is covered with reddish dust and rocks.

JUPITER

Length of day: 9.9 Earth hours
Length of year: 11.86 Earth years
Special features: The Great Red Spot, a giant storm that is larger than Earth

SATURN

Length of day: 10.7 Earth hours
Length of year: 29.46 Earth years
Special features: Bright rings made of chunks of ice that speed round it

► Colours have been added to this picture of Saturn to show its many separate rings.

14 Jupiter and Saturn are giants of the Solar System. Neither has a solid surface – they are made of mainly gas and liquid. Jupiter is the largest planet. It has stripy clouds and a huge storm called the Great Red Spot. Saturn is surrounded by rings made of icy chunks that orbit it.

15 Uranus and Neptune are furthest from the Sun. They are icy cold because they get so little heat from the Sun. Both are completely covered with deep clouds.

16 A growing number of dwarf planets, smaller than the main planets, are being discovered. Pluto is a dwarf planet although it was originally the ninth planet. Ceres, which was called the largest asteroid, is another. The other three – Haumea, Makemake and Eris – are recent discoveries, and are so far away that we know very little about them.

URANUS

Length of day: 17.24 Earth hours
Length of year: 84 Earth years
Special features: Does not spin upright so it looks like it is rolling round the Sun

NEPTUNE

Length of day: 16.1 Earth hours
Length of year: 165 Earth years
Special features: The strongest winds in the Solar System blow icy clouds round the planet

I DON'T BELIEVE IT!

The Earth is speeding round the Sun at 29.8 kilometres a second – more than 100,000 kilometres an hour. That's about 100 times faster than a jet airliner!

► White clouds float above dark storms that come and go on Neptune's blue cloudy surface.

Starry skies

17 People have always been fascinated by the stars and Moon. Ancient people watched the Sun cross the sky during the day and disappear at night. Then when it got dark they saw the Moon and stars move across the sky. They wondered what caused these things to happen.

18 Sometimes the Sun goes dark in the middle of the day. This is called a solar eclipse, and it is caused by the Moon moving in front of the Sun, blocking its light. People in the past did not know this, so eclipses were scary. In ancient China, people thought they were caused by a dragon eating the Sun.

19 In ancient times people did not know what the Sun, Moon and stars were. Many thought the Sun was a god. The ancient Egyptians called this god Ra. They believed he rode across the sky in a boat each day and was swallowed by the sky goddess, Nut, every evening and then born again the next morning.

▲ The Egyptians pictured their sky goddess Nut with a starry body and their sun god Ra sitting on a throne.

◀ Ancient Chinese people fired arrows and banged pots and pans during eclipses, believing this would frighten the dragon away.

▲ The Bayeux Tapestry, made during the 1070s, shows people pointing at the famous Halley's comet (at the top right).

▶ The Greek sun god, Helios, rode across the sky in a chariot pulled by four horses.

20 Early astronomers could not predict when comets would appear. Comets were known as 'long-haired stars' because of their glowing tails, and many people thought they brought bad luck. They were blamed for disasters, from floods and famines to defeat in battle.

▶ Quetzalcoatl was a feathered serpent, and to the Aztec people of Central America he was the god of the morning star.

Mapping the stars

21 Ancient astronomers made maps of star patterns, dividing them into groups called constellations. People around the world all grouped the stars differently. Today, astronomers recognize 88 constellations that cover the whole sky.

▼ Old star maps showed the constellations as animals such as Draco the Dragon and Ursa Minor the Little Bear.

▼ The northern half of the Earth has different constellations from the southern half, but all the star patterns stay the same night after night.

NORTHERN HEMISPHERE

Ophiuchus (Serpent Bearer)
Aquila (Eagle)
Hercules (Strongman)
Sagitta (Arrow)
Equuleus (Foal)
Serpens (Serpent)
Lyra (Lyre)
Corona Borealis (Northern Crown)
Delphinus (Dolphin)
Boötes (Herdsman)
Draco (Dragon)
Cygnus (Swan)
Pegasus (Winged Horse)
Coma Berenices (Berenice's Hair)
Lacerta (Lizard)
Virgo (Virgin)
Canes Venatici (Hunting Dogs)
Cepheus (King)
Andromeda (Chained Princess)
Pisces (Fishe
Leo (Lion)
Ursa Minor (Little Bear)
Cassiopeia (Queen)
Triangulum (Triangle)
Ursa Major (Great Bear)
Leo Minor (Little Lion)
Camelopardalis (Giraffe)
Aries (Ram)
Lynx (Lynx)
Perseus (Hero)
Hydra (Sea Serpent)
Cancer (Crab)
Auriga (Charioteer)
Cetus (Whale)
Gemini (Twins)
Taurus (Bull)
Orion (Hunter)
Canis Minor (Little Dog)

22 Astronomers gave names to the star patterns. Some are named after animals, including a bear, a lion, a swan, a dove, a crab and a snake. Others are named after gods and heroes. These include Orion (a hunter), Casseiopia (a queen), and the hero Perseus saving Princess Andromeda.

24 Stars appear to move across the sky at night. This is because the Earth is spinning all the time, but in the past people thought the stars were fixed to the inside of a huge hollow ball called the celestial sphere, which moved slowly around the Earth.

23 Over 2000 years ago, the Greek astronomer Hipparchus made a catalogue of over 850 stars. He listed their brightness and positions, and called the brightest ones first magnitude stars. Astronomers still call the brightness of a star its magnitude.

SPOT A STAR PATTERN

You will need:
clear night warm clothes dark place good view of the sky

If you live in the North, look for the saucepan-shape of the Big Dipper – four stars for the bowl and three for the handle.

If you live in the South, look overhead for four stars in the shape of a cross – the Southern Cross.

SOUTHERN HEMISPHERE

Lepus (Hare)
Canis Major (Great Dog)
Columba (Dove)
Eridanus (River Eridanus)
...ans ...ant)
Puppis (Stern), Carina (Keel) and Vela (Sail)
Caelum (Chisel)
Pictor (Painter's Easel)
Fornax (Furnace)
Dorado (Goldfish)
Phoenix (Phoenix)
Cetus (Whale)
Hydra (Sea Serpent)
Recticulum (Net)
Volans (Flying Fish)
...rater ...Cup)
Crux (Southern Cross)
Chamaeleon (Chameleon)
Grus (Crane), Tucana (Toucan), and Pavo (Peacock)
Centaurus (Centaur)
Musca (Fly)
Apus (Bird of Paradise)
...us ...v)
Triangulum Australe (Southern Triangle)
Indus (Indian)
Aquarius (Water Carrier)
...irgo ...irgin)
Ara (Altar)
Corona Australis (Southern Crown)
Piscis Austrinus (Southern Fish)
Scorpius (Scorpion)
Capricornus (Sea Goat)
Libra (Scales)
Serpens (Serpent) and Ophiuchus (Serpent Bearer)
Sagittarius (Archer)

25 Ancient astronomers noticed that one star seems to stay still while the others circle around it. This is the Pole Star. It is above the North Pole and shows which direction is north. The ancient Egyptians used this knowledge to align the sides of the pyramids exactly.

Keeping time

26 The Sun, Moon and stars can be used to measure time. It takes a day for the Earth to spin round, and a year for it to circle the Sun. By observing changes in the positions of constellations, astronomers worked out the length of a year so they could make a calendar.

27 It takes 29.5 days for the Moon to circle the Earth. The Moon seems to change shape because we see different amounts of its sunlit side as it goes round the Earth. When the sunlit side faces Earth we see a Full Moon. When it faces away, we see only a thin crescent shape.

Day 1

Day 3
Crescent
Moon

Day 5

Day 7
Half Moon

Day 10

Day 14
Full Moon

Day 17

Day 19

Day 21
Half Moon

Day 24

Day 26
Crescent
Moon

Day 28
New Moon

▲ The Moon's changing shapes are called the phases of the Moon. It doesn't really change shape – it is always a round ball of rock.

28 **Ancient people used sundials to tell the time.** A sundial consists of an upright rod and a flat plate. When the Sun shines, the rod casts a shadow on the plate. As the Sun moves across the sky, the shadow moves round the plate. Marks on the plate indicate the hours.

29 **As the Earth circles the Sun, different stars appear in the sky.** This helped people predict when seasons would change. In ancient Egypt the bright star Sirius showed when the river Nile would flood, making the land ready for crops.

▼ The shadow made by this sundial points to the time, which is marked on the round dial.

◄ Stonehenge's huge upright stones are lined up with sunrise on the longest day in midsummer and on the shortest day in midwinter.

30 **Stonehenge is an ancient monument in England that is lined up with the Sun and Moon.** It is a circle of giant stones over 4000 years old. It may have been used as a calendar, or an observatory to predict when eclipses would happen.

Wandering stars

31 When people began to study the stars they spotted five that were unlike the rest. Instead of staying in fixed patterns, they moved across the constellations, and they did not twinkle. Astronomers called them planets, which means 'wandering stars'.

32 The planets are named after ancient Roman gods. Mercury is the messenger of the gods, Venus is the god of love, Mars is the god of war, Jupiter is king of the gods and Saturn is the god of farming. Later astronomers used telescopes to find two more planets, and named them Uranus and Neptune after the gods of the sky and the sea.

33 At first people thought that the Earth was at the centre of everything. They believed the Sun, Moon and planets all circled the Earth. The ancient Greek astronomer Ptolemy thought the Moon was nearest Earth, then Mercury and Venus, then the Sun, and finally Jupiter and Saturn.

▼ Ptolemy's picture of the Solar System shows the Earth in the middle and the Sun and planets moving round it in circles.

DRAW AN ELLIPSE

You will need:
two drawing pins   paper
thick card   pencil   string

1. Place the paper on the card. Push the pins into the paper, placing them a little way apart.
2. Tie the string into a loop that fits loosely round the pins.
3. Using the pencil point, pull the string tight into a triangle shape.
4. Move the pencil round on the paper, keeping the string tight to draw an ellipse.

34
Astronomers measured the positions and movements of the planets. What they found did not fit Ptolemy's ideas. In 1543, the Polish astronomer Nicolaus Copernicus suggested that the planets circled the Sun. This explained much of what the astronomers saw, but still didn't fit the measurements exactly.

◀ Nicolaus Copernicus' view placed the Sun in the middle with the Earth moving round it with the other planets.

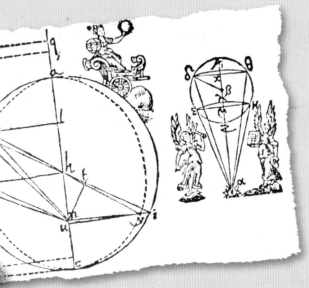

▲ Kepler's drawing shows how he worked out that the planets move along ellipses, not circles.

35
German astronomer Johannes Kepler published his solution to this problem in 1609. He realized that the orbits of Earth and the planets were not perfect circles, but ellipses (slightly squashed circles). This fitted all the measurements and describes the Solar System as we know it today.

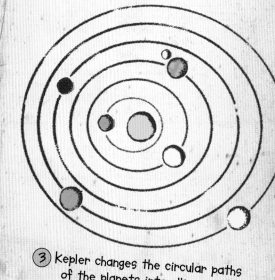

① From above, Ptolemy's plan shows everything (from inside to outside: Earth's Moon, Mercury, Venus, Sun, Mars, Jupiter, Saturn) moving round the Earth.

② Copernicus' view changes this to show everything moving round the Sun.

③ Kepler changes the circular paths of the planets into ellipses.

First telescopes

36 **The telescope was invented in about 1608.** Telescopes use two lenses (discs of glass that bulge out in the middle, or curve inwards) – one at each end of a tube. When you look through a telescope, distant things look nearer and larger.

37 **Italian scientist Galileo built a telescope in 1609.** He was one of the first people to use the new invention for astronomy. With it, Galileo observed craters and mountains on the Moon, and discovered four moons circling the planet Jupiter. He was also amazed to see many more stars in the sky.

▲ Galileo shows a crowd of people the exciting new things he can see through his telescope.

JUPITER

IO

EUROPA

Mirror

38 **When Galileo looked at the planet Venus through his telescope he saw that it sometimes appeared to be crescent shaped, just like the Moon.** This meant that Venus was circling the Sun and not the Earth and helped to prove that Copernicus was right about the planets circling the Sun. Galileo described his amazing discoveries in a book called *The Starry Messenger*.

▲ Jupiter's four largest moons are called the Galilean moons, because Galileo was the first person to see them using his telescope.

CALLISTO

GANYMEDE

39 Other astronomers were soon trying to build more powerful telescopes. In 1668, English scientist Isaac Newton made one in which he replaced one of the lenses with a curved mirror, shaped like a saucer. He had invented the reflecting telescope. Large modern telescopes are based on Newton's invention.

Eyepiece

Sliding focus

Ball mounting

I DON'T BELIEVE IT!
According to legend, Newton began to think about gravity when he saw an apple fall from a tree, and wondered why the apple fell to the ground instead of floating up.

40 Newton also worked out why the planets orbit the Sun. He realized that something was pulling the planets towards the Sun – a pulling force called gravity. The pull of the Sun's gravity keeps the planets in their orbits, and the Earth's gravity holds the Moon in its orbit. It also prevents everything on Earth from floating off into space.

◄ The mirror in Newton's telescope gave a clearer image of the stars than telescopes with lenses.

Discoveries with telescopes

▶ Halley's comet was last seen in 1986 and will return again in 2061.

41 Astronomers made many new discoveries with their telescopes. The English astronomer Edmund Halley was interested in comets. He thought that a bright comet seen in 1682 was the same as one that was seen in 1607, and predicted that it would return in 1758. His prediction was right and the comet was named after him – Halley's Comet.

◀ Halley also mapped the stars and studied the Sun and Moon.

▼ The Orion Nebula, a huge glowing cloud of gas, is Messier's object number 42.

42 The French astronomer Charles Messier was also a comet hunter. In 1781 he tried to make his search easier by listing over 100 fuzzy objects in the sky that could be mistaken for comets. Later astronomers realized that some of these are glowing clouds of dust and gas and others are distant galaxies.

▲ Messier's object number 16 is the Eagle Nebula, a dusty cloud where stars are born.

▼ Messier's object number 31 is a giant spiral galaxy called Andromeda.

43 William Herschel, a German astronomer living in England, discovered a new planet in 1781. Using a reflecting telescope he had built himself, he spotted a star that seemed to move. It didn't look like a comet, and Herschel realized that it must be a new planet. It was the first planet discovered with a telescope and was called Uranus.

▲ William Herschel worked as astronomer for King George III of England.

44 Astronomers soon discovered that Uranus was not following its expected orbit. They thought another planet might be pulling it off course. Following predictions made by mathematicians, astronomers found another planet in 1846. It was called Neptune. It is so far away that it looks like a star.

45 The discovery of Neptune didn't fully explain Uranus' orbit. In 1930 an American astronomer, Clyde Tombaugh, found Pluto. It was the ninth planet from the Sun and much smaller than expected. In 2006 astronomers decided to call Pluto a dwarf planet.

▲ Herschel's great telescope was the largest telescope in the world at the time and its mirror measured 1.2 metres across.

QUIZ

1. Who discovered the planet Uranus?
2. When was Halley's Comet last seen?
3. Which was the ninth planet from the Sun until 2006?

Answers:
1. William Herschel 2. 1986 3. Pluto

How telescopes work

46 **Telescopes make distant things look nearer.** Most stars are so far away that even with a telescope they just look like points of light. But the Moon and planets seem much larger through a telescope – you can see details such as craters on the Moon and cloud patterns on Jupiter.

47 **A reflecting telescope uses a curved mirror to collect light.** The mirror reflects and focuses the light. A second, smaller mirror sends the light out through the side of the telescope or back through a hole in the big mirror to an eyepiece lens. Looking through the eyepiece lens you see a larger image of the distant object.

▶ Star light bounces off the main mirror of a reflecting telescope back up to the eyepiece lens near the top.

Eyepiece lens

Reflected light

Secondary mirror

Light enters

Primary mirror

48 **A telescope that uses a lens instead of a mirror to collect light is called a refracting telescope.** The lens focuses the light and it goes straight down the telescope tube to the eyepiece lens at the other end. Refracting telescopes are not as large as reflecting ones because large lenses are very heavy.

Focused light

Eyepiece lens

49 Astronomers are building telescopes with larger and larger mirrors. Bigger mirrors reveal fainter objects so telescopes can see further and further into the Universe. They also show more details in the distant galaxies and the wispy glowing clouds between the stars.

50 Today, professional astronomers don't look through their telescopes. They use cameras to capture the images. A camera can build up an image over a long time. The light adds up to make a brighter image, showing things that could not be seen by just looking through the telescope.

▲ A telescope reveals round craters on the Moon and large dark patches called 'seas' although the Moon is completely dry.

Primary lens

Light enters

▼ In a refracting telescope the main lens at the top bends the light, making an image near the bottom of the telescope.

▲ The mirror from the Rosse Telescope in Ireland is 1.8 metres across and is kept in the Science Museum in London. One hundred years ago it was the largest telescope in the world.

I DON'T BELIEVE IT!
The Liverpool telescope on the island of La Palma in the Atlantic Ocean is able to automatically observe a list of objects sent to it via the Internet.

Telescopes today

51 **All large modern telescopes are reflecting telescopes.** To make clear images, their mirrors must be exactly the right shape. The mirrors are made of polished glass, covered with a thin layer of aluminium to reflect as much light as possible. Some are made of thin glass that would sag without supports beneath to hold it in exactly the right shape.

52 **Large telescope mirrors are often made up of many smaller mirrors.** The mirrors of the Keck telescopes in Hawaii are made of 36 separate parts. Each has six sides, which fit together to make a mirror 10 metres across – about the width of a tennis court. The small mirrors are tilted to make exactly the right shape.

53 **The air above a telescope is constantly moving.** This can make their images blurred. Astronomers reduce this by using an extra mirror that can change shape. A computer works out what shape this mirror needs to be to remove the blurring effect and keeps changing it every few seconds. This is called adaptive optics.

▶ A huge frame holds the mirrors of a large reflecting telescope in position while tilting and turning to point at the stars.

Light enters

Secondary mirror

Reflected light

Primary mirror

Frame

▲ The main mirror of the Gran Telescopio Canarias telescope measures 10.4 metres across when all its 36 separate parts are fitted together.

55
Large telescopes can work together to see finer detail than a single telescope. When the two Keck telescopes are linked, they produce images that are almost as good as a telescope with a mirror as wide as the distance between them – 85 metres, (about the length of a football field).

54
Telescopes must be able to move to track the stars. It may take hours to make an image of a very faint, distant target and during this time the target will move gradually across the sky. Motors drive the telescope at just the right speed to keep it pointing at the target. All the time the image is being recorded using CCDs like those in an ordinary digital camera.

QUIZ
1. What are telescope mirrors made of?
2. How many sides does each piece of a Keck telescope mirror have?
3. Why do telescopes have to move?

Answers:
1.Glass 2. 6
3. To track the stars

▶ This picture of Saturn was taken by one of the Keck telescopes. The orange colours have been added to show the different temperatures in its clouds and rings.

Observatories

TRUE OR FALSE?

1. Observatories are built close to large cities for convenience.
2. The volcano that the Mauna Kea observatory is built on is dormant.
3. Chile is a good place to build observatories because it rains a lot.

Answers:
1. False 2. True 3. False

56 **Observatories are places for watching the skies, often where telescopes are built and housed.** There are usually several telescopes of different sizes at the same observatory. Astronomers choose remote places far away from cities, as bright lights would spoil their observations.

57 **Observatories are often on the tops of mountains and in dry desert areas.** This is because the air close to the ground is constantly moving and full of clouds and dust. Astronomers need very clear, dry, still air so they build their telescopes as high as possible above most of the clouds and dust.

▶ The Gemini North telescope is one of the telescopes at the Mauna Kea Observatories in Hawaii. It has a twin called Gemini South in Chile, South America.

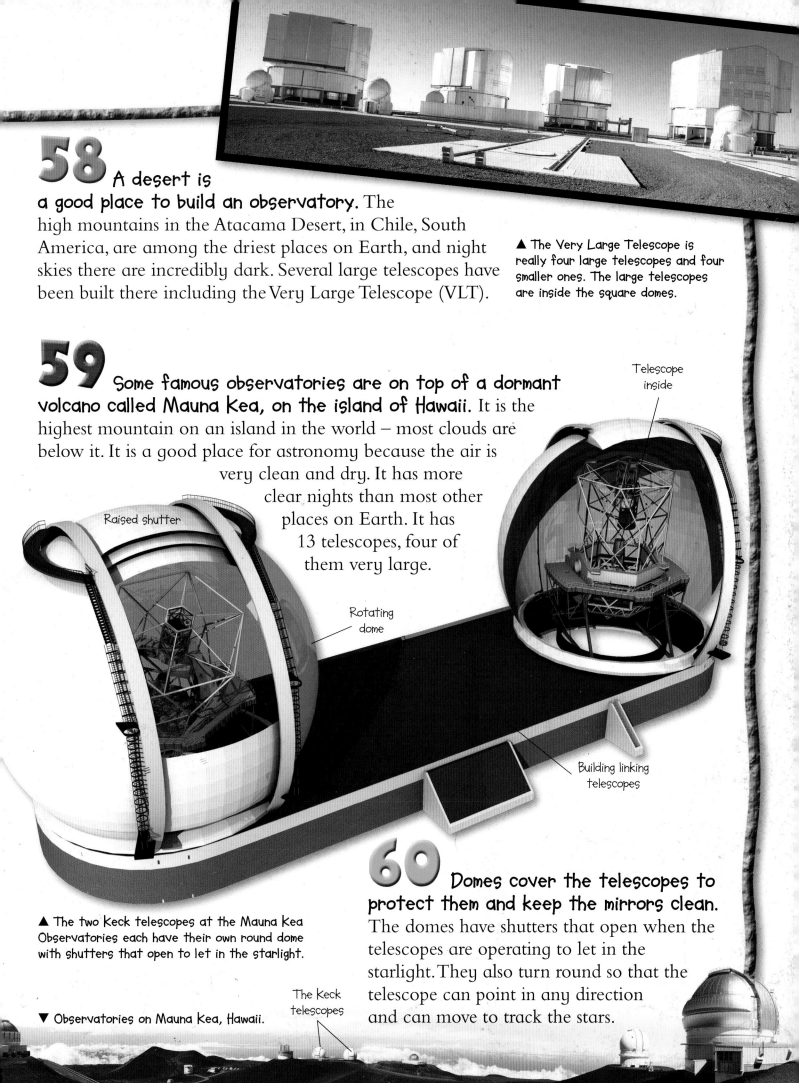

58
A desert is a good place to build an observatory. The high mountains in the Atacama Desert, in Chile, South America, are among the driest places on Earth, and night skies there are incredibly dark. Several large telescopes have been built there including the Very Large Telescope (VLT).

▲ The Very Large Telescope is really four large telescopes and four smaller ones. The large telescopes are inside the square domes.

59
Some famous observatories are on top of a dormant volcano called Mauna Kea, on the island of Hawaii. It is the highest mountain on an island in the world – most clouds are below it. It is a good place for astronomy because the air is very clean and dry. It has more clear nights than most other places on Earth. It has 13 telescopes, four of them very large.

Telescope inside

Raised shutter

Rotating dome

Building linking telescopes

▲ The two Keck telescopes at the Mauna Kea Observatories each have their own round dome with shutters that open to let in the starlight.

▼ Observatories on Mauna Kea, Hawaii.

The Keck telescopes

60
Domes cover the telescopes to protect them and keep the mirrors clean. The domes have shutters that open when the telescopes are operating to let in the starlight. They also turn round so that the telescope can point in any direction and can move to track the stars.

Splitting light

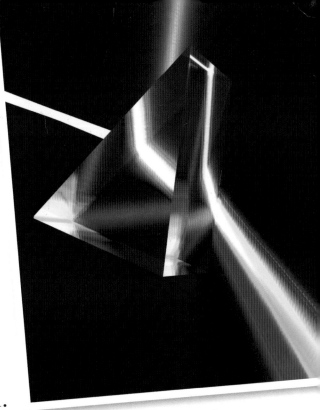

61 Astronomers find out about distant stars by studying the starlight that reaches Earth. They can get more data from the light by splitting it into its different colours – like a rainbow that forms when rain drops split up sunlight. These colours are called a spectrum.

▲ White light going in one side of a wedge-shaped glass prism spreads out into a rainbow of colours, making a spectrum.

RAINBOW SPECTRUM

You will need:
drinking glass   small mirror
water   torch   card

1. Put the mirror in the glass so that it faces upwards.
2. Pour water into the glass to cover the mirror.
3. In a dark room, shine the torch onto the mirror.
4. Hold the card to catch the reflected light from the mirror and see a rainbow – the water and mirror have split the light into a spectrum.

62 Astronomers can tell how hot a star is from its spectrum. The hottest are blue-white, the coolest are red, and in between are yellow and orange stars. The spectrum also shows how big and bright the star is so astronomers can tell which are ordinary stars and which are red giants or supergiants.

63 A star's spectrum can show what gases the star is made of. Each gas has a different pattern of lines in the spectrum. Astronomers can also use the spectrum to find out which different gases make up a cloud of gas, by looking at starlight that has travelled through the cloud.

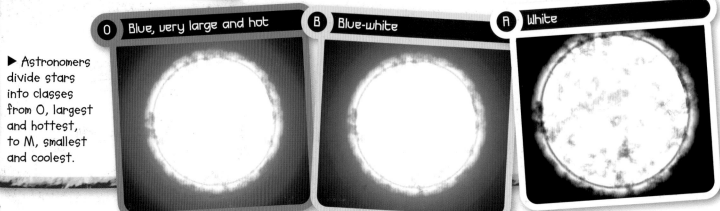

▶ Astronomers divide stars into classes from O, largest and hottest, to M, smallest and coolest.

O Blue, very large and hot
B Blue-white
A White

64 If a star or galaxy is moving away from Earth, its light is stretched out. This shows up in its spectrum and astronomers call it red shift. They use it to work out how fast a galaxy is moving and how far away it is. If the galaxy is moving towards Earth, the light gets squashed together and shows up in its spectrum as blue shift.

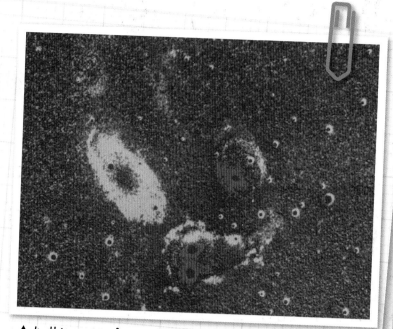

▲ In this group of galaxies, called Stephan's Quintet, the ones that have been coloured red are moving away very quickly.

▼ This diagram shows the light waves coming to Earth from a distant galaxy as a wiggly line.

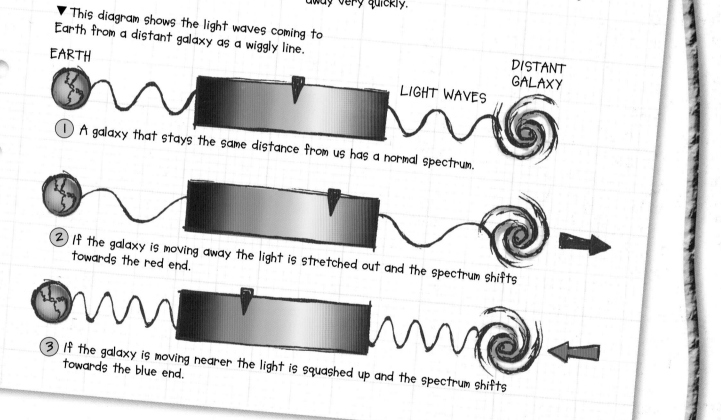

EARTH

DISTANT GALAXY

LIGHT WAVES

① A galaxy that stays the same distance from us has a normal spectrum.

② If the galaxy is moving away the light is stretched out and the spectrum shifts towards the red end.

③ If the galaxy is moving nearer the light is squashed up and the spectrum shifts towards the blue end.

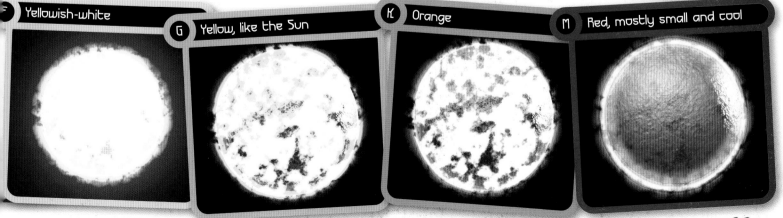

| F Yellowish-white | G Yellow, like the Sun | K Orange | M Red, mostly small and cool |

Space telescopes

65 Galaxies and stars send out other kinds of radiation, as well as light. Some send out radio waves like the ones that carry TV signals. There are also X-rays, like the kind that hospitals use to show broken bones, infrared light, gamma rays and ultra-violet light. They all carry information.

66 Some kinds of radiation are detected more easily by telescopes in space. This is because the air around Earth stops most radiation from reaching the ground, which is good, because it would be harmful to life on Earth. Space telescopes orbit Earth to collect the radiation and send the information down to Earth.

67 The Hubble space telescope is like a normal telescope, but it is above the air. Its images are much clearer than if it were on the ground. It has produced images of distant gas clouds showing star birth, and looked deep into space at galaxies that have never been seen before.

▶ The Hubble space telescope was launched into orbit around the Earth in 1990 and is still sending astronomers amazing images from space.

QUIZ
1. What kind of radiation can spot newborn stars?
2. Which space telescopes collect gamma rays from space?
3. What kind of radiation can spot black holes?

Answers:
1. Infrared radiation
2. The Fermi and Integral Gamma-ray Telescopes 3. X-rays and gamma rays

This picture includes data from Hubble (coloured green and dark blue), Spitzer (coloured red) and Chandra (coloured pale blue).

68
The space telescopes Chandra X-ray Observatory and XMM Newton both collect X-rays. The X-rays come from very hot gas inside huge galaxy clusters. They also reveal black holes, because gas swirling around black holes gets so hot that it gives out X-rays.

◀ For over ten years the Chandra X-ray Observatory has orbited the Earth looking at black holes and exploding stars.

69
Infrared light is picked up by the Spitzer and Herschel space telescopes. It comes from cool stars and clouds of dust and gas. Infrared light can be used to see through dust clouds around newborn stars, and around young stars where new planets may be forming. It also reveals the centre of our galaxy, which is hidden by dust.

▶ The Spitzer space telescope must be kept very cold so it can pick out the infrared light from distant galaxies.

70
The Fermi Gamma-ray Space Telescope and Integral are telescopes that collect gamma rays. These rays come from violent events in space such as huge explosions when stars blow up or collide. Like X-rays, gamma rays can also reveal black holes.

Radio telescopes

71 Radio waves from space are collected by radio telescopes. Most radio waves can travel through the air, so these telescopes are built on the ground. But there are lots of radio waves travelling around the Earth, carrying TV and radio signals, and phone calls. These can all interfere with the faint radio waves from space.

72 Radio telescopes work like reflecting telescopes, but instead of using a mirror, waves are collected by a big metal dish. They look like huge satellite TV aerials. Most dishes can turn to point at targets anywhere in the sky, and can track targets moving across the sky.

▶ Each radio telescope dish in the Very Large Array measures 25 metres across and can tilt and turn to face in different directions.

73 We can't see radio waves, but astronomers turn the signals into images we can see. The images from a single radio telescope dish are not very detailed but several radio telescopes linked together can reveal finer details. The Very Large Array (VLA) in New Mexico, USA, has 27 separate dishes arranged in a 'Y' shape, all working together as though it was one huge dish 36 kilometres across.

▶ These two orange blobs are clouds of hot gas on either side of a galaxy. They are invisible to ordinary telescopes but radio telescopes can reveal them.

74 Radio waves come from cool gas between the stars. This gas is not hot enough to glow so it can't be seen by ordinary telescopes. Radio telescopes have mapped clouds of gas showing the shape of the Milky Way Galaxy. They have also discovered what seems to be a massive black hole at its centre.

75 Radio waves reveal massive jets of gas shooting out from distant galaxies. The jets are thrown out by giant black holes in the middle of some galaxies, which are gobbling up stars and gas around them.

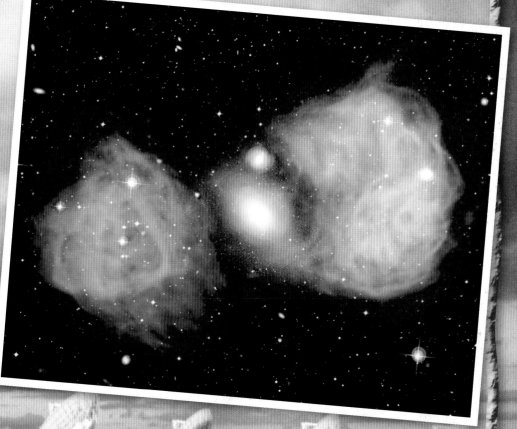

Watching the Sun

76 The Sun is our closest star and astronomers study it to learn about other stars. Without the Sun's light and heat nothing could live on the Earth, so astronomers keep a close eye on it. Tongues of very hot gas called flares and prominences often shoot out from the Sun.

▼ A loop of glowing gas called a prominence ❶ arches away from the Sun. Sun spots ❷ look dark because they are cooler that the rest of the surface.

77 Particles constantly stream out from the surface of the Sun in all directions. This is called the solar wind. Sometimes a huge burst of particles, called a Coronal Mass Ejection (CME), breaks out. If one comes towards Earth it could damage satellites and even telephone and power lines. CMEs can be dangerous for astronauts in space.

78 There are often dark patches on the Sun. These are cooler areas, and are called sunspots. The number of sunspots changes over time. Every 11 years numbers increase to a maximum of 100 or more, then in between the numbers go down to very few, or even none.

① Wispy gas surrounds the Sun (coloured blue) in this image from the SOHO spacecraft. ② SOHO captures a Coronal Mass Ejection exploding out from the Sun.

79 **A spacecraft called SOHO has been watching the Sun since 1995.** It orbits the Sun between the Earth and the Sun, sending data and images back to Earth. It warns of changes in solar wind and of CMEs that could hit Earth, and has spotted many comets crashing into the Sun.

I DON'T BELIEVE IT!
The Sun is losing weight! Every second about 4 million tonnes of its gas is turned into energy and escapes as light and heat. The Sun is so big that it can continue losing weight at this rate for about another 5 billion years.

80 **STEREO are a pair of spacecraft that look at the Sun.** They orbit the Sun, one each side of the Earth, to get a 3D view. Like SOHO, they are looking for storms on the Sun that could affect the Earth. Information from STEREO is helping astronomers to work out why these storms happen.

▶ This illustration shows the two Stereo spacecraft soon after they were launched in 2006. They moved apart until they were on either side of the Earth.

The edge of the Universe

81 Astronomers think that the Universe started in a huge explosion they call the Big Bang. They know that distant galaxies are all moving further apart so the Universe must have been squashed tightly together billions of years ago. They think that some kind of explosion sent everything flying apart about 13.7 billion years ago.

82 As astronomers look further away they are also looking back in time. This is because light takes time to travel across the vast distances in space. It takes over four years for light to reach Earth from the second-nearest star (after the Sun), so we see this star as it was when the light left it four years ago. Light can take billions of years to travel from distant galaxies, so astronomers are looking back at the Universe as it was billions of years ago.

❹ Our Sun and the Solar System formed after about 9 billion years

❸ Stars and galaxies appeared after about 200–600 million years

9 billion yrs

❷ After 300,000 years atoms started to form

300 million yrs

300,000 yrs

❶ The Universe was unimaginably hot and tiny at first but cooled as it expanded

▶ This shows the Universe as it expanded and changed from the Big Bang to the present day.

83 Astronomers have found faint radiation coming from all over the sky. They call this the Cosmic Background Radiation. It is the remains of radiation left by the Big Bang explosion and helps to prove that the Big Bang really happened. Astronomers send satellites up to map this radiation and find out more about the Universe when it was very young.

13.7 billion yrs

⑤ The Universe is now about 13.7 billion years old

▲ These galaxies are so far away that we are seeing them as they were billions of years ago when the Universe was much younger.

84 Astronomers use their biggest telescopes and space telescopes to try and find the most distant galaxies. They do not know how soon after the Big Bang the first stars and galaxies appeared and whether they were different from the stars and galaxies they see today. The Hubble space telescope has taken images of very faint faraway galaxies showing astronomers what the early Universe was like.

Up close

85 The planets and our Moon have all been explored by space probes. These travel through space carrying cameras and other instruments with which they can gather data. They then send all the information and images back to astronomers on Earth.

QUIZ

I. How many planets did the Voyager 2 space probe visit?
2. Did the *Spirit* and *Opportunity* rovers find running water on Mars?
3. How did the *Magellan* space probe map Venus?

Answers:
1. Four 2. No – but they found signs that there may have been some long ago 3. It used radar to 'see' through the clouds

86 Some space probes fly past planets, gathering information. The *Voyager 2* space probe flew past the four giant planets (Jupiter, Saturn, Uranus and Neptune) in turn between 1979 and 1989. Astronomers now know much more about these planets from the detailed information and images *Voyager 2* sent back.

VOYAGER 2

▶ *Voyager 2 sent back this picture of Callisto, one of Jupiter's large moons.*

Launch date: 20 August, 1977
Mission: Flew past Jupiter in 1979, Saturn in 1981, Uranus in 1986 and Neptune in 1989. Now flying out of the Solar System into deep space.

87

Space probes can orbit a planet to study it for longer. The probe *Cassini* went into orbit round Saturn. It carried a smaller probe that dropped onto Saturn's largest moon, Titan, to look at its surface, which is hidden by cloud. The main probe circled Saturn, investigating its moons and rings.

88

Venus is hidden by clouds, but the *Magellan* probe was able to map its surface. The probe sent radio signals through the clouds to bounce off the surface. It then collected the return signal. This is called radar. It revealed that Venus has many volcanoes.

CASSINI

▶ Saturn and its rings, taken by the *Cassini* spacecraft as it approached the planet.

Launch date: 15 October, 1997
Mission: Arrived at Saturn in 2004. Dropped Huygens probe onto Saturn's largest moon, Titan, then went into orbit to explore Saturn, its rings and moons.

SPIRIT AND OPPORTUNITY

89

Some probes land on a planet's surface. The probes *Spirit* and *Opportunity* explored the surface of Mars. They move slowly, stopping to take pictures and analyze rocks. They have discovered that although Mars is very dry now, there may have once been water on the surface.

Launch date: 10 June, 2003 (Spirit) and 7 July, 2003 (Opportunity)
Mission: After landing on Mars in January 2004 the two rovers drove across the surface testing the rocks and soil and sending back images and data.

▲ Among the many rocks scattered across the dusty Martian landscape *Spirit* found a rock that could have crashed down from space.

Astronomy from home

90 **Many people enjoy astronomy as a hobby.** You need warm clothes and somewhere dark, away from street and house lights, and a clear night. After about half an hour your eyes adjust to the dark so you can see more stars. A map of the constellations will help you find your way around the night sky.

91 **Binoculars reveal even more stars and show details on the Moon.** It is best to look at the Moon when it is half full. Craters, where rocks have crashed into the Moon, show up along the dark edge down the middle of the Moon. Binoculars also show Jupiter's moons as spots of light on or either side of the planet.

92 **Telescopes are usually more powerful than binoculars and show fainter stars.** They also show more detail in faint gas clouds called nebulae. Amateurs use reflecting and refracting telescopes, mounted on stands to keep them steady.

93 **A camera can be fixed to a telescope to photograph the sky.** A camera can build up an image over time if the telescope moves to follow the stars. The images show details that you could not see by just looking through the telescope.

KIT LIST

* Star map
* Red light torch
* Deckchair
* Warm clothes
* Pencil and notebook
* Blanket or sleeping bag
* Binoculars
* Telescope

SPOT VENUS

Venus is the brightest planet and easy to spot – it is known as the 'evening star'. Look towards the west in the twilight just after the Sun has set. The first bright 'star' to appear will often be Venus.

▲ In 1997 the bright Comet Hale Bopp could be seen easily without a telescope or binoculars.

▼ In November each year amateur astronomers look out for extra shooting stars during the Leonid meteor shower.

94 Meteors, also called shooting stars, look like streaks of light in the sky. They are made when tiny pieces of space rock and dust hit the air around the Earth and burn up. Several times during the year there are meteor showers when many shooting stars are seen. You can spot meteors without a telescope or binoculars.

95 Amateurs can collect useful information for professional astronomers. They are often the first to spot a new comet in the sky. Comets are named after the person who found them and some amateur astronomers even specialize in comet-spotting. Others watch variable stars and keep records of the changes in their brightness.

▶ An amateur astronomer uses binoculars to see the many stars in the Milky Way.

96 **Kepler is a new satellite built specially to look for stars that might have planets where there could be life.** So far, astronomers have not found life anywhere else in the Solar System. Kepler was launched in 2009 and is looking at stars to see if any of them have any planets like Earth.

► A Delta II rocket launches the Kepler spacecraft in March 2009 on its mission to hunt for distant planets.

I DON'T BELIEVE IT!

Astronomers are planning a new radio telescope, to be built in either Australia or South Africa. It is called the Square Kilometre Array and will have at least 3000 separate radio telescopes. It should start working in 2020.

97 **ALMA (short for Atacama Large Millimetre Array) is a powerful new radio telescope being built high up in the Atacama Desert in Chile.** When it is complete in 2012 it will have 66 radio dishes linked together to make one huge radio telescope.

98 The James Webb Space Telescope will replace the Hubble Space telescope in 2014. Its mirror will be 6.5 metres across, nearly three times wider than Hubble's main mirror. This will not fit in a rocket so it will be made of 18 separate mirrors that will unfold and fit together once the telescope is in space.

▲ A large sunshield will keep the mirrors of the James Webb telescope cool so it can make images using infrared light.

99 Several new giant telescopes are being planned. The Thirty Meter Telescope will have a mirror 30 metres across — about the length of three double-decker buses. This will be made of 492 smaller mirrors. The European Extremely Large Telescope will have an even larger mirror, 42 metres across, made of 984 separate mirrors. Both should be ready to use in 2018.

100 A new X-ray telescope is planned for launch in 2021. The International X-ray observatory will look at what happens near black holes and astronomers hope it will show black holes in young galaxies billions of years ago.

▲ The European Extremely Large Telescope will be the largest optical telescope in the world when it is built in the Atacama Desert in Chile.

Index

Entries in **bold** refer to main subject entries; entries in *italics* refer to illustrations.